Business Plan Template

Complete Fill in the Blanks Sample Business Plan Proposal

(With MS Word Version, Excel Spreadsheets, and 7 Free Gifts)

MEIR LIRAZ

Published by BizMove
www.bizmove.com

Table of Contents

1. Complete Fill In The Blanks Business Plan Template

(A MS Word version of this template is included in the free bonuses section in chapter 5 - use it to prepare and customize your own business plan)

A business plan serves several purposes. It can help convince investors or lenders to finance your business. It can persuade partners or key employees to join your company. Most importantly, it serves as a roadmap guiding the launch and growth of your new business.

Writing a business plan is an opportunity to carefully think through every step of starting your company so you can prepare for success. This is your chance to discover any weaknesses in your business idea, identify opportunities you may not have considered, and plan how you will deal with challenges that are likely to arise. Be honest with yourself as you work through your business plan. Don't gloss over potential problems; instead, figure out solutions.

A good business plan is clear and concise. A person outside of your industry should be able to understand it. Avoid overusing industry jargon or terminology.

Most of the time involved in writing your plan should be

spent researching and thinking. Make sure to document your research, including the sources of any information you include.

Avoid making unsubstantiated claims or sweeping statements. Investors, lenders and others reading your plan will want to see realistic projections and expect your assumptions to be supported with facts.

This template includes instructions for each section of the business plan, followed by corresponding fillable worksheet/s.

The last section in the, instructions, "Refining Your Plan," explains ways you may need to modify your plan for specific purposes, such as getting a bank loan, or for specific industries, such as retail.

Proofread your completed plan (or have someone proofread it for you) to make sure it's free of spelling and grammatical errors and that all figures are accurate.

Business Plan

[Insert Date]

Company name

Street address 1

Street address 2

City, state, ZIP

Business phone

Website URL

Email address

Confidentiality Agreement

The undersigned reader acknowledges that any information provided by _____ in this business plan, other than information that is in the public domain, is confidential in nature, and that any disclosure or use of same by the reader may cause serious harm or damage to _____. Therefore, the undersigned agrees not to disclose it without express written permission from

_____.

Upon request, the undersigned reader will immediately return this document to

_____.

_____
Signature

_____
Name (typed or printed)

_____
Date

This is a business plan. It does not imply an offering of securities.

Table of Contents

I. Instructions: Executive Summary

The Executive Summary is the most important part of your business plan. Often, it's the only part that a prospective investor or lender reads before deciding whether or not to read the rest of your plan. It should convey your enthusiasm for your business idea and get readers excited about it, too.

Write your Executive Summary LAST, after you have completed the rest of the business plan. That way, you'll have thought through all the elements of your startup and be prepared to summarize them.

The Executive Summary should briefly explain each of the below.

1. **An overview of your business** idea (one or two sentences).
2. **A description of your product and/or service.** What problems are you solving for your target customers?
3. **Your goals for the business.** Where do you expect the business to be in one year, three years, five years?
4. **Your proposed target market.** Who are your ideal customers?
5. **Your competition and what differentiates your business.** Who are you up against, and what unique selling proposition will help you succeed?
6. **Your management team and their prior experience.** What do they bring to the table that will give your business a competitive edge?

7. **Financial outlook for the business.** If you're using the business plan for financing purposes, explain exactly how much money you want, how you will use it, and how that will make your business more profitable.

Limit your Executive Summary to one or two pages in total.

After reading the Executive Summary, readers should have a basic understanding of your business, should be excited about its potential, and should be interested enough to read further.

After you've completed your business plan, come back to this section to write your executive summary on the next page.

Executive Summary

(Write after you've completed the rest of the business plan.)

II. Instructions: Company Description

This section explains the basic elements of your business. Include each of the below:

1. **Company mission statement**
    A mission statement is a brief explanation of your company's reason for being. It can be as short as a marketing tagline (*"MoreDough is an app that helps consumers manage their personal finances in a fun, convenient way"*) or more involved: (*"Doggie Tales is a dog daycare and grooming salon specializing in convenient services for urban pet lovers. Our mission is to provide service, safety and a family atmosphere, enabling busy dog owners to spend less time taking care of their dog's basic needs and more time having fun with their pet."*) *In general, it's best to keep your mission statement to one or two sentences.*

2. **Company philosophy and vision**
    a. What values does your business live by? *Honesty, integrity, fun, innovation* and *community* are values that might be important to your business philosophy.
    b. *Vision* refers to the long-term outlook for your business. What do you ultimately want it to become? For instance, your vision for your doggie day-care center might be to become a national chain, franchise or to sell to a larger company.

3. **Company goals**
    Specify your long- and short-term goals as well as any milestones or benchmarks you will use to measure your progress. For instance, if one of your goals is to open a

second location, milestones might include reaching a specific sales volume or signing contracts with a certain number of clients in the new market.

4. **Target market**
   You will cover this in-depth in the Marketing Plan section. Here, briefly explain who your target customers are.

5. **Industry**
   Describe your industry and what makes your business competitive: Is the industry growing, mature or stable? What is the industry outlook long-term and short-term? How will your business take advantage of projected industry changes and trends? What might happen to your competitors and how will your business successfully compete?

6. **Legal structure**
   a. Is your business a sole proprietorship, LLC, partnership or corporation? Why did you choose this particular form of business?
   b. If there is more than one owner, explain how ownership is divided. If you have investors, explain the percentage of shares they own. This information is important to investors and lenders.

After reading the Company Description, the reader should have a basic understanding of your business's mission and vision, goals, target market, competitive landscape and legal structure.

Use the Company Description worksheet on the next page to help you complete this section.

Company Description Worksheet

Business Name	
Company Mission Statement	
Company Philosophy/ Values	
Company Vision	
Goals & Milestones	1. 2. 3.
Target Market	
Industry/ Competitors	1. 2. 3.
Legal Structure/ Ownership	

III. Instructions: Products & Services

This section expands on the basic information about your products and services included in the Executive Summary and Company Description. Explain in detail each of the below:

1. **Your company's products and/or services:** What do you sell, and how is it manufactured or provided? Include details of relationships with suppliers, manufacturers and/or partners that are essential to delivering the product or service to customers.
2. **The problem the product or service solves**: Every business needs to solve a problem that its customers face. Explain what the problem is and how your product or service solves it. What are its benefits, features and unique selling proposition? Yours won't be the only solution (every business has competitors), but you need to explain why your solution is better than the others, targets a customer base your competitors are ignoring, or has some other characteristic that gives it a competitive edge.
3. **Any proprietary features that give you a competitive advantage**: Do you have a patent on your product or a patent pending? Do you have exclusive agreements with suppliers or vendors to sell a product or service that none of your competitors sell? Do you have the license for a product, technology or service that's in high demand and/or short supply?
4. **How you will price your product or service**: Describe the pricing, fee, subscription or leasing structure of your product or service. How does your product or service fit into the competitive landscape in terms of pricing—are you on the low end, mid-range or

high end? How will that pricing strategy help you attract customers? What is your projected profit margin?

Include any product or service details, such as technical specifications, drawings, photos, patent documents and other support information, in the Appendices.

After reading the Products & Services section, the reader should have a clear understanding of what your business does, what problem it solves for customers, and the unique selling proposition that makes it competitive.

Use the Product and Service Description Worksheet on the next page to help you complete this section.

Product & Service Description Worksheet

Business Name	
Product/ Service Idea	
Special Benefits	
Unique Features	
Limits and Liabilities	
Production and Delivery	
Suppliers	
Intellectual Property Special Permits	
Product/ Service Description	

IV. Instructions: Marketing Plan

This section provides details on your industry, the competitive landscape, your target market and how you will market your business to those customers.

Market research

There are two kinds of research: *primary* and *secondary*. *Primary* market research is information you gather yourself. This could include going online or driving around town to identify competitors; interviewing or surveying people who fit the profile of your target customers; or doing traffic counts at a retail location you're considering.

Secondary market research is information from sources such as trade organizations and journals, magazines and newspapers, Census data and demographic profiles. You can find this information online, at libraries, from chambers of commerce, from vendors who sell to your industry or from government agencies.

This section of your plan should explain:

- The total size of your industry
- Trends in the industry – is it growing or shrinking?
- The total size of your target market, and what share is realistic for you to obtain
- Trends in the target market – is it growing or shrinking? How are customer needs or preferences changing?

Barriers to entry

What barriers to entry does your startup face, and how do you plan to overcome them? Barriers to entry might include:

- High startup costs
- High production costs
- High marketing costs
- Brand recognition challenges
- Finding qualified employees
- Need for specialized technology or patents
- Tariffs and quotas
- Unionization in your industry

Threats and opportunities

Once your business surmounts the barriers to entry you mentioned, what additional threats might it face? Explain how the following could affect your startup:

- Changes in government regulations
- Changes in technology
- Changes in the economy
- Changes in your industry

Use the SWOT Analysis Worksheet on the next page to identify your company's weaknesses and potential threats, as well as its strengths and the potential opportunities you plan to exploit.

SWOT Analysis Worksheet

	Strengths	Weaknesses	Opportunities	Threats
Product/ Service Offering				
Brand/ Marketing				
Staff/HR				
Finance				
Operations/ Management				
Market				

Can any of your strengths help with improving your weaknesses or combating your threats? If so, please describe how below.

Based on the information above, what are your immediate goals/next steps?

Based on the information above, what are your long-term goals/next steps?

Product/service features and benefits

Describe all of your products or services, being sure to focus on the customer's point of view. For each product or service:

- Describe the most important features. What is special about it?
- Describe the most important benefits. What does it do for the customer?

In this section, explain any after-sale services you plan to provide, such as:

Product delivery

Warranty/guarantee

Service contracts

Ongoing support

Training

Refund policy

Target customer

Describe your target customer. (This is also known as the *ideal customer* or *buyer persona.*)

You may have more than one target customer group. For instance, if you sell a product to consumers through distributors, such as retailers, you have at least two kinds of target customers: the distributors (businesses) and the end users (consumers).

Identify your target customer groups, and create a demographic profile for each group that includes:

For consumers:

Age

Gender

Location

Income

Occupation

Education level

For businesses:

 Industry

Location

Size

Stage in business (startup, growing, mature)

Annual sales

Key competitors

One of the biggest mistakes you can make in a business plan is to claim you have "no competition." Every business has competitors. Your plan must show that you've identified yours and understand how to differentiate your business. This section should:

List key companies that compete with you (including names and locations), products that compete with yours and/or services that compete with yours. Do they compete across the board, or just for specific products, for certain customers or in certain geographic areas?

Also include indirect competitors. For instance, if you're opening a restaurant that relies on consumers' discretionary spending, then bars and nightclubs are indirect competitors.

Use the Competitor Data Collection Plan on the next page to brainstorm ways you can collect information about competitors in each category.

Competitor Data Collection Plan

Price		
Benefits/Features		
Size/profitability		
Market strategy		

Once you've identified your major competitors, use the Competitive Analysis Worksheet on the next page to compare your business to theirs.

Competitive Analysis Worksheet

For each factor listed in the first column, assess whether you think it's a strength or a weakness (S or W) for your business and for your competitors. Then rank how important each factor is to your target customer on a scale of 1 to 5 (1 = very important; 5 = not very important). Use this information to explain your competitive advantages and disadvantages.

Factor	Me	Competitor A	Competitor B	Competitor C	Importance to Customer
Products					
Price					
Quality					
Selection					
Service					
Reliability					
Stability					
Expertise					
Company Reputation					
Location					
Appearance					
Sales Method					
Credit Policies					
Advertising					
Image					

Positioning/Niche

Now that you've assessed your industry, product/service, customers and competition, you should have a clear understanding of your business's niche (your unique segment of the market) as well as your positioning (how you want to present your company to customers). Explain these in a short paragraph.

How you will market your product/service

In this section, explain the marketing and advertising tactics you plan to use.

Advertising may include:

- Online
- Print
- Radio
- Cable television
- Out-of-home

Which media will you advertise in, why and how often?

Marketing may include:

- Business website
- Social media marketing
- Email marketing
- Mobile marketing
- Search engine optimization

- Content marketing
- Print marketing materials (brochures, flyers, business cards)
- Public relations
- Trade shows
- Networking
- Word-of-mouth
- Referrals

What image do you want to project for your business brand?

What design elements will you use to market your business? (This includes your logo, signage and interior design.) Explain how they'll support your brand.

Promotional budget

How much do you plan to spend on the marketing and advertising outreach above:

- Before startup (These numbers will go into your startup budget)
- On an ongoing basis (These numbers will go into your operating plan budget)

Use the Marketing Expenses Strategy Chart on the next page to help figure out the cost of reaching different target markets.

Marketing Expenses Strategy Chart

	Target Market 1	Target Market 2	Target Market 3
One-Time Expenses			
Monthly or Annual Expenses			
Labor Costs			

Pricing

You explained pricing briefly in the "Products & Services" section; now it's time to go into more detail. How do you plan to set prices? Keep in mind that few small businesses can compete on price without hurting their profit margins. Instead of offering the lowest price, it's better to go with an average price and compete on quality and service.

- Does your pricing strategy reflect your positioning?
- Compare your prices with your competitors'. Are they higher, lower or the same? Why?
- How important is price to your customers? It may not be a deciding factor.
- What will your customer service and credit policies be?

Use the Pricing Strategy Worksheet on the next page to help with your pricing.

Pricing Strategy Worksheet

Business Name	
Which of the following pricing strategies will you employ? Circle one.	

Cost Plus	Value Based	Other:
The costs of making/ obtaining your product or providing your service, plus enough to make a profit	*Based on your competitive advantage and brand (perceived value)*	

Provide an explanation of your pricing model selection.

Include strategy info on your major product lines/service offerings. List industry/market practices and any considerations to be discussed with your mentor.

Location or proposed location

If you have a location picked out, explain why you believe this is a good location for your startup.

If you haven't chosen a location yet, explain what you'll be looking for in a location and why, including:

- Convenient location for customers
- Adequate parking for employees and customers
- Proximity to public transportation or major roads
- Type of space (industrial, retail, etc.)
- Types of businesses nearby

Focus on the location of your building, not the physical building itself. You'll discuss that later, in the Operations section.

Distribution channels

What methods of distribution will you use to sell your products and/or services? These may include:

- Retail
- Direct sales
- Ecommerce
- Wholesale
- Inside sales force
- Outside sales representatives
- OEMs

If you have any strategic partnerships or key distributor

relationships that will be a factor in your success, explain them here.

If you haven't yet finalized your distribution channels, use the <u>*Distribution Channel Assessment Worksheet*</u> *on the next page to assess the pros and cons of each distribution channel you are considering.*

Distribution Channel Assessment Worksheet

	Distribution Channel 1	Distribution Channel 2	Distribution Channel 3
Ease of Entry			
Geographic Proximity			
Costs			
Competitors' Positions			
Management Experience			
Staffing Capabilities			
Marketing Needs			

12-month sales forecast

Create a month-by-month sales projection for 12 months.

If you've already made some sales, you can use those as a basis for your projections. If, like most startups, you haven't sold anything yet, you'll need to create estimates based on your market research, your proposed marketing strategies and your industry data.

Create two forecasts: a "best guess" scenario (what you really expect) and a "worst case" scenario (one you're confident you can reach no matter what).

Keep notes on the research and assumptions that go into developing these sales forecasts. Financing sources will want to know what you based the numbers on.

After reading the Marketing Plan section, the reader should understand who your target customers are, how you plan to market to them, what sales and distribution channels you will use, and how you will position your product/service relative to the competition.

V. Instructions: Operational Plan

This section explains the daily operation of your business, including its location, equipment, personnel and processes.

Production

How will you will produce your product or deliver your service? Describe your production methods, the equipment you'll use and how much it will cost to produce what you sell.

Quality control

How will you maintain consistency? Describe the quality control procedures you'll use.

Location

Where is your business located? You briefly touched on this in the Company Overview. In this section, expand on that information with details such as:

a. The size of your location
b. The type of building (retail, industrial, commercial, etc.)
c. Zoning restrictions
d. Accessibility for customers, employees, suppliers and transportation if necessary
e. Costs including rent, maintenance, utilities, insurance and any buildout or remodeling costs
f. Utilities

Legal environment

What type of legal environment will your business operate in? How are you prepared to handle legal requirements? Include details such as:

g. Any licenses and/or permits that are needed and whether you've obtained them

h. Any trademarks, copyrights or patents that you have or are in the process of applying for
i. The insurance coverage your business requires and how much it costs
j. Any environmental, health or workplace regulations affecting your business
k. Any special regulations affecting your industry
l. Bonding requirements, if applicable

Personnel

What type of personnel will your business need? Explain details such as:

m. What types of employees? Are there any licensing or educational requirements?
n. How many employees will you need?
o. Will you ever hire freelancers or independent contractors?
p. Include job descriptions.
q. What is the pay structure (hourly, salaried, base plus commission, etc.)?
r. How do you plan to find qualified employees and contractors?
s. What type of training is needed and how will you train employees?

Inventory

If your business requires inventory, explain:

- What kind of inventory will you keep on hand (raw materials, supplies, finished products)?

- What will be the average value of inventory (in other words, how much are you investing in inventory)?
- What rate of inventory turnover do you expect? How does this compare to industry averages?
- Will you need more inventory than normal during certain seasons? (For instance, a retailer might need additional inventory for the holiday shopping season.)
- What is your lead time for ordering inventory?

Suppliers

List your key suppliers, including:

- Names, addresses, websites
- Type and amount of inventory furnished
- Their credit and delivery policies
- History and reliability
- Do you expect any supply shortages or short-term delivery problems? If so, how will you handle them?
- Do you have more than one supplier for critical items (as a backup)?
- Do you expect the cost of supplies to hold steady or fluctuate? If the latter, how will you deal with changing costs?
- What are your suppliers' payment terms?

Credit policies

If you plan to sell to customers on credit, explain:

- Whether this is typical in your industry (do customers expect it)?

- What your credit policies will be. How much credit will you extend? What are the criteria for extending credit?
- How will you check new customers' creditworthiness?
- What credit terms will you offer?
- Detail how much it will cost you to offer credit, and show that you've built these costs into your pricing structure.
- How will you handle slow-paying customers? Explain your policies, such as when you will follow up on late payments, and when you will get an attorney or collections agency involved.

After reading the Operational Plan section, the reader should understand how your business will operate on a day-to-day basis.

VI. Instructions: Management & Organization

This section should give readers an understanding of the people behind your business, their roles and responsibilities, and their prior experience. If you're using your business plan to get financing, know that investors and lenders carefully assess whether you have a qualified management team.

1. **Biographies**
   Include brief biographies of the owner/s and key employees. Include resumes in the Appendix. Here, summarize your experience and those of your key employees in a few paragraphs per person. Focus on the prior experience and skills that have prepared your team to succeed in this business. If anyone has previous experience starting and growing a business, explain this in detail.

2. **Gaps**
   Explain how you plan to fill in any gaps in management and/or experience. For instance, if you lack financial know-how, will you hire a CFO or retain an accountant? If you don't have sales skills, will you hire an in-house sales manager or use outside sales reps?

3. **Advisors**
   List the members of your professional/advisory support team, including:
      a. Attorney

b. Accountant
c. Board of directors
d. Advisory board
e. Insurance agent
f. Consultants
g. Banker
h. Mentors and other advisors

If they have experience or specializations that will increase your chances of success, explain. For instance, does your mentor have experience launching and growing a similar business?

4. Organization Chart
   Develop and include an organization chart. This should include both roles that you've already filled and roles you plan to fill in the future.

After reading the Management & Organization section, the reader should feel confident that you have a qualified team leading your business.

Use the Management Worksheet and Organization Chart on the next two pages to highlight your management team.

Management Worksheet

Bio/s	
Gaps in Management or Experience	
Advisors	

VII. Instructions: Startup Expenses & Capitalization

In this section, detail the expenses involved in opening for business and how much capital you'll need. (Do not include ongoing expenses after your business opens; those are listed in the Financial Plan.) Estimating startup expenses as accurately as possible helps you gather enough startup capital.

1. **Start-Up Expenses**

   Download and complete the Start-Up Expenses template (included in the MS Word version of this template, featured in chapter 5 (b). In working on this Business Plan, you should already have gathered most, if not all, of the information you need. In the body of this section, be sure to explain all of the assumptions behind the figures. How did you come up with these expenses? If you've secured or expect to secure loans, explain the source/s, amount/s and terms. If you've secured or expect to secure investors, explain how much each investor will contribute and what percentage of ownership each receives in return.

   Be sure to include extra capital for unexpected expenses. Opening a new business almost always ends up costing more than expected, and you need to be prepared. List this figure in the Start-Up Expenses template under "Reserve for Contingencies." How much should you set aside for contingencies? You can talk to other business owners in your industry to get a ballpark figure. If you can't come up with a figure this way, a good rule of thumb is to set aside 20% to 25% of your total startup costs for contingencies.

2. **Opening Day Balance Sheet**
    Download and complete the Opening Day Balance
    Sheet (included in the MS Word version of this
    template, featured in chapter 5 (b). Use it to detail the
    expected state of your business finances on opening
    day. As with the Start-Up Expenses sheet, be sure to
    explain the assumptions behind the figures.

3. **Personal Financial Statement**
    If you are using the business plan to seek financing,
    include personal financial statements for each owner
    and each major stockholder. The personal financial
    statements should detail each person's assets and
    liabilities outside of the business and their personal net
    worth. Investors and/or lenders typically expect
    business owners to use personal assets to finance a
    startup, and they'll want to see how much capital you
    have available from your personal finances.

After reading the Startup Expenses & Capitalization
section, the reader should know how much money is
needed to start the business and how well capitalized you
are.

VIII. Instructions: Financial Plan

Your financial plan is perhaps the most important element of your business plan. Lenders and investors will review it in detail. Developing your financial plan helps you set financial goals for your startup and assess its financing needs. Include the following:

1. **12-month profit & loss projection**
   Also known as an *income statement* or *P&L*, the 12-month profit and loss projection is the centerpiece of your business plan. Download the 12-Month Profit and Loss Projection (included in the MS Word version of this template, featured in chapter 5 (b) and fill in your projected sales, cost of goods sold and gross profit. (Refer to the Sales Forecast you created in Section IV). Then list your expenses, net profit before taxes, estimated taxes and net operating income.

   Be sure to explain the assumptions behind the numbers in your P&L. Keep detailed notes about how you came up with these figures; you may need this information to answer questions from potential financing sources.

2. **Optional: 3-year profit & loss projection**
   A three-year profit and loss projection is not essential to a business plan. However, you may want to create one if you expect your business's financials to change substantially after the first year, or if investors or lenders require it. Download the 3-Year Profit and Loss Projection template (included in the MS Word version

of this template, featured in chapter 5 (b), and use it to create your projection.

3. **Cash flow projection**
   The cash flow statement tracks how much cash your business has on hand at any given time. Once your business is up and running, you'll want to keep close tabs on your cash flow statement. For now, however, you're creating a cash flow *projection*. Think of the cash flow projection as a forecast for your business checking account. It details when you need to spend money on things such as inventory, rent and payroll, and when you expect to receive payments from customers and clients. For example, you may make a sale, have to buy inventory to fulfill the sale, and not collect payment from the customer for 30, 60 or 90 days. The cash flow projection takes these factors into account, helping you budget for upcoming expenses so your business doesn't run out of money.

   Download the 12-Month Cash Flow Statement (included in the MS Word version of this template, featured in chapter 5 (b) and use it to create your projections.

4. **Optional: 3-year cash flow statement**
   Depending on your needs and the purpose of your business plan, you may also want to include a 3-year cash flow statement. If so, download the 3-Year Cash Flow Statement (included in the MS Word version of this template, featured in chapter 5 (b), and use it to create your projections. This is a much simpler

document than the 12-month cash flow statement, but can still be useful in making plans.

5. **Projected balance sheet**

   A balance sheet subtracts the company's liabilities from its assets to arrive at the owner's equity. You already created an opening day balance sheet in Section 1. Now, download the Balance Sheet - Projected, (included in the MS Word version of this template, featured in chapter 5 (b), and create a projected balance sheet showing the estimated financial condition of your business at the end of its first year. The major difference between the two is that the projected balance sheet includes any owner's equity resulting from the business's first year in operation. Lenders and investors may want to see this projection.

6. **Break-even calculation**

   The break-even analysis projects the sales volume you need in order to cover your costs. In other words, when will the business break even? Download the Break-Even Analysis template (included in the MS Word version of this template, featured in chapter 5 (b), and, using your profit and loss projections, enter your expected fixed and variable costs. Adjust the categories to reflect your own business.

   You can even create a couple of different break-even analyses for different scenarios. For example, your payroll costs will vary depending on whether you hire full-time employees or use independent contractors. Creating different break-even analyses can help you determine the best option.

7. **Use of capital**
   If you're using the business plan to seek financing from lenders or investors, provide a breakdown of how you will the capital and what results you expect. For example, perhaps you will use the money to buy new equipment and expect that to double your production capacity.

After reading the Financial Plan section, the reader should understand the assumptions behind your financial projections and be able to judge whether these projections are realistic.

IX. Instructions: Appendices

Don't slow your readers down by cluttering your business plan with supporting documents, such as contracts or licenses. Instead, put these documents in the Appendices, and refer to them in the body of the plan so readers can find them if needed.

Below are some elements many business owners include in their Appendices.

1. Agreements (Leases, contracts, purchase orders, letters of intent, etc.)
2. Intellectual property (trademarks, licenses, patents, etc.)
3. Resumes of owners/key employees
4. Advertising/marketing materials
5. Public relations/publicity
6. Blueprints/plans
7. List of equipment
8. Market research studies
9. List of assets that can be used as collateral

You can also include any other materials that will give readers a fuller picture of your business or support the projections and assumptions you make in your plan. For instance, you might want to include photos of your proposed location, illustrations or photos of a product you are patenting, or charts showing the projected growth of your market.

After reviewing the Appendices, the reader should feel satisfied that the assumptions throughout the plan are backed up by documentation and evidence.

X. Instructions: Refining the Plan

Modify your business plan for your specific needs, audience and industry. Here are some guidelines to help:

For Raising Capital from Bankers

Bankers want to know that you'll be able to repay the loan. If the business plan is for bankers or other lenders, include:
- How much money you're seeking
- How you'll use the money
- How that will make your business stronger
- Requested repayment terms (number of years to repay)
- Any collateral you have and a list of all existing liens against your collateral

For Raising Capital from Investors

Investors are looking for dramatic growth, and they expect to share in the rewards. If the business plan is for investors, include:
- Investment amount you need short-term
- Investment amount you'll need in two to five years
- How you'll use the money and how that will help your business grow
- Estimated return on investment
- Exit strategy for investors (buyback, sale or IPO)
- Percentage of ownership you will give investors
- Milestones or conditions you will accept
- Financial reporting you will provide to investors

- How involved investors will be on the board or in management

For a Manufacturing Business

- Explain the operations involved in manufacturing your product/s.
- What equipment is needed? What are the production/capacity limits of the equipment?
- What are the production/capacity limits of the proposed physical plant?
- Is specialized labor needed?
- What raw materials do you need for manufacturing? Are there any special requirements for storing these?
- What quality control procedures will you use?
- How will you manage inventory levels?
- What is your supply chain?
- Explain any new products you're developing, or products you plan to begin developing after startup.

For a Service Business

- Explain your prices and the methods used to set them.
- What systems and processes will you use for ensuring consistent delivery of services?
- What quality control procedures will you use?
- How will you measure employee productivity?
- Will you subcontract any work to other businesses? If so, what percentage of work will be subcontracted? Will you make a profit on subcontracting?

- Explain your credit, payment and collections policies and procedures.
- How will you maintain your client base and get long-term contracts?
- **Explain any new services you're developing or services you plan to add after startup.**

For a Retail Business

- List specific brands you plan to carry that will give you a competitive advantage.
- How will you manage inventory? What inventory management software will you use?
- What forms of payment will you accept? What payment processing service will you use?
- What point-of-sale software and hardware will you use?
- Explain your markup policies. Your prices should be profitable, competitive and in line with your brand.
- Initial inventory level: Find the industry average annual inventory turnover rate (available in the RMA book). Multiply your initial inventory investment by the average turnover rate. The result should be at least equal to your projected first year's cost of goods sold. If not, you may need to budget more for startup inventory.
- What are your customer service policies?
- How will you handle returns and exchanges?
- Will your retail store also have an ecommerce site, or is one planned for the future?

For an Ecommerce Business

- Will you sell a physical product, a service, a digital product (such as eBooks) or some combination of these?
- If you're selling physical products, how will you brand and package them?
- Will you sell on your own website, online marketplaces (such as Amazon) or both?
- What technology providers and platforms will you use to run your ecommerce site?
  - Web hosting service
  - Web design service
  - Shopping cart provider
  - Payment processing service
  - Fulfillment & shipping services
  - Email marketing services
- Can the solutions you've chosen quickly scale up or down as needed?
- Where will you get your products? Will you manufacture them in-house, buy them from manufacturers or use drop shippers?
- How will you handle returns and exchanges?
- What are your customer service policies? How will you provide customer service?
- Will you use any proprietary technology of your own and if so, what advantages does that give you?

For a Software or SaaS business

- What is your pricing structure? Will you use a free trial, "freemium" or paid business model?

- If you offer free services or a free trial option, how will you upsell customers to a payment model? What percentage of customers are expected to become paying customers?
- Have you tested your software? Are any "early adopters" already using the product?
- How will you encourage long-term contracts in order to create recurring revenues?
- How will you manage rapidly changing markets, technologies and costs?
- How will you keep your company competitive?
- Will you use in-house developers or outsource this function?
- How will you provide customer support?
- How will you retain key personnel?
- Are you using any proprietary or exclusive software that will give you a competitive edge?
- How will you protect your intellectual property?
- What additional products or updates to current products are you planning after launch?

Now That You're (Almost) Finished . . .

Remember to go back, and complete the Executive Summary.

2. Sample Business Plan

Here is an abbreviated example of a serious sample business plan examples template proposal. It is provided to give you a feeling for the style of writing that is used in a business plan, and is not intended to be a comprehensive guide of what should be covered in a good plan.

The humorous content of this business plan example is supplied only for the readers interest. For optimum effectiveness, care should be taken to minimize the humorous content in an actual proposal.

Free Sample Business Plan Examples
Table Of Contents

Statement of Funding Proceeds

Executive Summary

Description Of The Business

The Market

Marketing Strategy

Business Location

Licenses/Permits/Registrations

Insurance/Bonding/Employee Benefits

Management

Personnel

Financial Data

Appendix

Statement Of Funding Proceeds

Children's World has developed a line of toys that are superior to all other products that exist on the market today. In order to service our identified target markets with these superior toys, significant capital infusion is required.

Specifically, the required $15,000,000 will be allocated appropriately to:

Marketing and Advertising $ 1,500,000

Salaries -0-

Facilities 50,000

Capital Equipment 450,000

Research and Development 1,000,000

Operational Expenses 2,000,000

Inventory 10,000,000

Total $15,000,000

Â Executive Summary

Children's World is the major player in the global gift giving industry. Originally founded as a sole proprietorship in 1930, the marketing tactics employed by Children's

World had grown to the level of being a family legend by 1940. Annual toy production of Children's World exceeded 86,000,000 units at this time, and major expansion plans were developed. However, due to a slight downturn in the global economy, these plans have been shelved as projected profit levels have fallen to a near break even point in 1993.

To revitalize the company, a rigorous program of research and development was undertaken in the early 1950's. The first major breakthrough of which is ready for production. To be able to make maximum use of our proprietary breakthrough technology, Children's World needs to upgrade its existing facilities, as well as reevaluate the company's sleigh delivery system It is anticipated that a late model Cessna Citation could be modified to meet the operating requirements of Children's World. In addition, several used cargo planes will need to be acquired to facilitate the development of large stockpiles of toys at strategic global locations. A central hub system is being considered.

Additional manufacturing upgrades are planned to facilitate the projected increases in manufacturing output. Some of the upgrades include the replacement of manual lathes with automated CNC machines, the installation of spray booths using the latest in electrostatic technology, computerized conveyor and sorting systems, and an upgrade in the Statistical Process Control (SPC) area of the Quality Assurance Department.

As can be seen, Children's World is now at a point where they need to seek outside funding to refurbish/renovate their production facilities, upgrade their global navigational equipment, establish a more visible image, and to establish an extensive line of credit to cover seasonal inventory expenses.

This loan will be backed by the full assets and inventory of the Children's World company. As the attached Balance Sheet indicates, these assets have a current valuation of $5,000,000. In addition, of the $15,000,000 requested, $10,450,000 will be spent on inventory and capital equipment which will also be used as collateral for the note. As the attached cash flows indicate, Children's World should be able to service the debt incurred by this loan application. It is anticipated that the Return On Investment (ROI) thrown off from this loan will be 200% adjusted on a yearly basis. Timing of the loan and the market entry of the product will be critical, however, with the maximum value occurring from a November entry.

Description Of The business

Our Mission at Children's World is: "To provide toys and games of exceptional quality, in a timely manner, priced at or below our competition, to enhance the profits of our company."

Background

Children's World is a sole proprietorship that was founded in 1930. It is wholly owned by Mr. and Mrs. Sanford Theodore Clause. For the past 50 years, Children's World has experienced an increase in the public awareness of our year end close-out (where we give away surplus inventory). Because of this practice, the public has begun to think of us on a seasonal basis as a philanthropic organization.

To alleviate this problem, we have just completed the development phase of a novel and proprietary product line that will once again place Children's World in the minds of the public on a daily basis. By 1940, our operation had produced 86,000,000 toys, and has operated profitably ever since. However, revenue projections for fiscal year xxxx, without external funding for the introduction of this new product line, is expected to be down to a break even level ($1,100). With the funding for the renovations, advertising, and new product line our profits are expected to reach $30,000,000. Annual growth is projected to be 21% per year through the year 2100.

Concept

The "state of the art" of the industry today dictates that toys are produced without ever being touched by human hands. Our new revolutionary product line capitalizes on the fact that our toys have traditionally been hand built by our local elf community. Although our production methods are slow in comparison to other manufacturers, our quality levels are high while our costs are kept very modest.

This new product line incorporates a rare, refined essence (known only to our advanced Research And Development Dept.) that causes a strong attraction to be formed between the toy and the customer who first sees the toy. This essence is well known in the animal community. For instance, it is the reason why ducklings bond to the first animal they see after emerging from their shell (commonly called "imprinting"). These ducklings will not physically allow themselves to be separated, to any significant distance, from the "parent" animal for approximately six months.

After lengthy collaboration with the local duck community, and extensive field testing (test population will not be disclosed), our top notch R&D staff has been able to identify and synthesize the essence and increase its strength. When incorporated into our line of toys, this essence will create a bond between the recipient and the toy that will last for one full year! During this time, like the ducklings, the recipient who first sees the toy will not want to be separated from the toy to any significant distance (typically less than fifteen feet).

This instant "imprinting" at the time of viewing the toy had initially placed our R&D staff in a considerable quandary. To be effective and "imprint" on only the intended recipient, the entire channel of distribution must not be able to see the product. This enigma was eventually resolved by the decision to place the product in an opaque wrapper, bag, etc. that could be given to the intended recipient to be "opened". To prevent the early opening of the wrapper/bag, we have developed several colorful prints that can be placed on the opaque wrapper thereby lending it an attractive external appearance.

Compared to competitors products, the use of the

"essence" will dramatically increase the recipients enjoyment of, and involvement with, our product line. Other significant refinements that our R&D staff has been able to develop are:

1. Gender Specific Essences. Using this innovation, a toy incorporating a female gender essence will bond most strongly with female recipients, and vice versa. This will help reduce the demand for pink and lavender trucks, baseball mitts, etc., and will dramatically reduce our internal manufacturing problems and inventory requirements.

2. Variable Time Factor Essences. This innovation will allow us to produce toys that have a "short" imprint time (30 - 90 days) for use when we need to spur sales, or a longer imprint time (up to 365 days) for a moderated sales level. We have found through extensive research that 330 days is optimal in that it allows for approximately one month of "de-imprinting" and subsequent anticipation build up among the recipients. Naturally, this will cause some friction among the family sub-units, but that can not be avoided if we are to develop a maximum market penetration.

Business plan example - The Market

The Children's World target market includes the pre-adolescent to young adult groups on a global scale. Using data supplied by the Bureau of the Census the total population of the world is estimated at 5,700,000,000. Of this basis group, we have conservatively placed our estimate of our total target market at slightly over 300 million customers. At the present time our sales are hovering at the 250,000,000 unit mark (up from 86,000,000 in 1940) giving us an 83.3% market share. We believe that the requested funding will allow us to increase this market share to roughly 95% over the next two years. This would increase our sales by an additional 35,000,000 units per year (see Appendix A for source information and calculations).

Our primary focus (and most of our extensive field testing) is on the 1-5 year old individual. Our products are gender specific, with male vs. female sales forecasts mirroring the population demographics. As our products gain acceptance within this market, we will move to expand into the teenage markets as this time frame is known for its friction between family sub-units. This will mask the effects of the "de-imprinting" irritations, and will aid us in minimizing any public disclosure (and competitor espionage) during the early phase of our market introduction.

All Children's World products are protected by the trademark and copyright laws, however we will not seek patent protection for the "essence" lines. Instead, we will keep these lines as a trade secret, thus preventing public disclosure and the subsequent possibility of legal entanglements from disgruntled parents, consumer activists, etc.

Initial responses from our market test customers indicate that our new lines are enjoying an excellent reaction. Inquiries from prospective customers suggest that there is considerable demand for these toys. Relationships with leading retailers, major accounts, and distributors substantiate the fitness of Children's World for considerable growth and accomplishment.

Competition

Although Children's World is a broad based manufacturing and transportation company, competitive threats today come primarily from other toy manufacturers. However, with 83.3% of the overall market, the competition does not play a significant role on company pricing/credit policies.

The major competitors that are facing Children's World are as follows:

Mattel, Inc. (Hawthorne, CA) Primarily a game manufacturer/marketer with sales of over $50,000,000/year.

Roadmaster Corp. (Olney, IL) Manufacturer of juvenile riding toys with sales of over $100,000,000/year.

Parker Brothers (Beverly, MA) Primarily a game manufacturer/marketer with sales of over $250,000,000/year.

Flexible Flyer Co. (West Point, MS) Manufacturer of juvenile riding toys with sales of over $50,000,000/year.

Tyco Toys, Inc. (Mount Laurel, NJ) Manufacturer of trucks/cars with sales of over $100,000,000/year.

Hasbro, Inc. (Pawtucket, RI) Primarily a game manufacturer/marketer with sales of over $50,000,000/year.

In spite of the competition in the toy industry, Children's World has continued to deliver a high quality, low cost product that is unique to this industry. In addition, our research indicates that our performance is superior to any other company on the market today.

The gift market is heavily seasonal, with the preponderance of sales coming late in the year. As stated in the "Background" section of the Business Description above, Children's World has experienced an increase in the public awareness of our year end close-out (where we give away surplus inventory). Because of this practice, the public has begun to think of us on a seasonal basis as a philanthropic organization.

It is our belief that we will be able to turn this mistaken perception around with the funds that we are seeking via this proposal. After all, in all comparisons Children's World's products provide more features and have superior performance than competitive products. In most cases, the difference in the number of features is substantial. A complete technical comparison is available upon request.

Marketing Strategy

The "state of the art" of the industry today dictates that toys are produced without ever being touched by human hands. Our new revolutionary product line capitalizes on the fact that our toys have traditionally been hand built by our local elf community. Although our production methods are slow in comparison to other manufacturers, our quality levels are high while our costs are kept very modest. In addition, the exciting new breakthroughs that we have achieved in our R&D department (see the Description of the Business section above) will further increase the sales and usage of our products.

To get the most out of our marketing dollars, we have developed the following strategy for promoting our products:

Pricing and Profitability. Our pricing is tied to our philosophy of operating at a break even basis. However, because of both the past losses incurred in the toy giveaways, and to pay for the capital improvements outlined in this plan, we will increase our pricing in order to retire the newly incurred debt. We are projecting a first year net profit of $30,000,000 as the result of this project.

Selling Tactics. Consistent with previous years, preseason publicity outlining new merchandising concepts is utilized extensively to generate paid advertising participation from retailers and shopping centers world wide. This has worked well, and we have no plans to alter this strategy.

Distribution. Central pre-distribution hubs have now been established in each country. This concept permits faster delivery, without the need to return to the North Pole each time the sleigh needs restocking. This is the most cost effective procedure implemented by Children's World in the last 50 years.

Advertising and Promotion. Cooperative advertising funds are available to all participating retailers which leverages our national advertising exposure 400%. Proof of advertising activity from the participating merchant in the form of a paid invoice from the merchant and a tear sheet from the print media is required for final payment.

Public Relations. This activity has outgrown our in-house capabilities. Therefore, we have retained the services of an international public relations firm, Good, Better and Best, Inc., to coordinate those activities. The firm provides us their services at cost, as they benefit measurably through their visibility and association with Children's World .

Business Relationships. Children's World participates heavily in trade shows during the Summer months. This activity permits us to maximize our efforts and focus on the major retailers and buyers. Promotional activity by retailers may need to be reviewed in the near future, as seasonal promotion once targeted exclusively for December, has been pushed backward to Thanksgiving, and on occasion is now occurring as early as Halloween. This is a concern we are reviewing with our public relations firm.

Credit Terms. Standard credit terms will be offered to wholesalers/retailers (2% 10 net 30), while cash and checks will be accepted on the retail level.

Business Plan Examples - Business Location

The Children's World production facilities wholly owned and are located at 101 North Pole Lane, Arctic Circle, Earth. Due to the nature of the toy industry, and its propensity for industrial espionage, Children's World decided at an early stage that steps must be taken to isolate and camouflage their facilities. To date, their efforts have been largely successful, although a few close calls have been noted.

The facilities are debt free and are kept in good repair by the local elf community. To accommodate the planned product line expansion, only minor renovations (approximately $50,000) will be necessary as stated in the "Statement of Funding Proceeds" section above.

To safeguard both their new and existing product lines, Children's World respectfully declines to provide detailed information on this subject heading.

Licenses/Permits/Registrations

All licenses, and permits required for the continued operation of the company have been either secured, or renewed. Due to our location, our company is not affected by zoning regulations.

All Children's World products are already protected by the appropriate trademark and copyright filings. Children's World will not seek patent protection for the "essence" lines, however. Instead, we will keep these lines as a trade secret, thus preventing public disclosure and the subsequent possibility of legal entanglements from disgruntled parents, consumer activists, etc.

FAA certification and flight tests of all pilots and craft are both current and comprehensive, and are on file with the proper authorities.

Insurance/Employee Benefits

Due to the unique nature of their work force and the isolation of the environment, Children's World does not have to provide insurance for their employees. However, Children's World does have full property insurance as well as a general liability insurance policy for $1,000,000 per the requirements of most retailers.

Employee benefits include unlimited supplies of aspirin, nasal decongestants, as well as other cold related medicines. Regarding vacation leave, Children's World provides two weeks of paid vacation each year. The company also their employees with equipment, lift passes, etc. free of charge for skiing, snowmobiling, snowshoeing, etc. However, no vacations are permitted during the months of October through December due to production demands.

Management

How we started

Children's World was founded in 1930 by Sanford Theodore Clause who recognized the entrepreneurial opportunities presented by the establishment of a charitable society. Through his efforts gift giving became more fashionable, particularly around the time of the Christian celebration of Christmas.

Management team

Our key management team consists of Mr. and Mrs. Clause whose backgrounds consist of almost 60 years of manufacturing and marketing experience. Our manufacturing team consists of over 300 well trained elf volunteers, each with at least 200 years of manufacturing, engineering and design experience.

A listing of our corporate organization is as follows:

Sanford T. Clause, President

Elizabeth M. Clause, Vice President, Henry J. Ticklebone, Director of Finance, Abagail B. Greenleaf, Director of Marketing Princely J. Rockafellow, Director of Sales, James A. Bronson, Director of Engineering, Jillaney P. Quackenmeyer, Director Research & Development' Jeremy C. McDougal, Director of Operations, Thistle P. Stickler, Corporate Attorney.

As stated above, the strength of Children's World management team stems from the combined expertise in both management and technical areas. This has produced outstanding results over the past 60 years.

The time honored leadership characteristics of Children's World's management team have resulted in broad and flexible goal setting -to meet the ever changing demands of the quickly moving marketplace requiring our products. This is evident when the team responds to situations requiring new and innovative capabilities.

Personnel

The following are the summary job descriptions for the key officers of the Children's World organization:

Abagail B. Greenleaf, Director of Marketing ($100,000/year salary) Manage market planning, advertising, public relations, sales promotion, merchandising and facilitate staff services. Identifying new markets and corporate scope and market research. Identify foreign markets.

Princely J. Rockafellow, Director of Sales ($100,000/year salary) Manage field sales organization, territories and quotas. Manage sales office activities including customer/product support/service.

Henry J. Ticklebone, Director of Finance ($150,000/year salary) Management of working capital including receivables, inventory cash and marketable securities. Financial forecasting, including capital budget, cash budget, proforma financial statements, external financing requirements, financial condition requirements.

James A. Bronson, Director of Engineering ($85,000/year salary) Oversees product development including quality control, physical distribution, product and packaging design, new product development improvement, and improvements on existing products. Research and development.

Jeremy C. McDougal, Director of Operations ($175,000/year salary) Service, manufacturing, raw materials management and allocation.

Outside support

An outside Board of Advisors, including highly qualified

business and industry professionals/experts from the elfin community, will assist our management team to make appropriate decisions and take the most effective action; however, they will not be responsible for management decisions.

At this time we do not forecast any need for extensive restructuring, and/or large scale hiring campaigns. Our expansion campaign will be able to be handled by our current staff of highly skilled employees.

Financial Data

Please see the attached financial projections including five years of historical financials, as well as a three year cash flow and income statement projection.

3. How to Develop a Results Driven Business Plan

There are many reasons why a business plan should be prepared. Each is sufficient by itself for why one must go through the exercise of preparing the actual business plan. This guide discusses free small business plans, business plan outline. Regardless of the specific reason, the underlying goal of preparing a business plan is to insure the success of the business. Here are the main reasons why a business plan should be prepared:

Provides you with the road map that you need in order to run your business. It allows you to make detours, change directions, and alter the pace that you set in starting or running the business.

To assist in financing. Whether one is starting up a small business or is an entrepreneur, banks and financial institutions want to see that you know where you are, where you are going, and how you are going to get there.

The plan will tell you how much money you need, when you will need it, and how you are going to get it. In other words, how you will do your financing?

Helps you to clearly think through what type of business you are starting, and allows you to consider every aspect of that business.

Raises the questions that you need to have answered in order to succeed in your business.

Establishes a system of checks and balances for your business so that you avoid mistakes.

Sets up bench marks to keep your business under control.

Helps you develop the competitive spirit to make you keenly prepared and ready to operate.

Makes you think through the entire business process so that you do not open the business blindly or lack vital information in opening and maintaining your business.

Forces you to analyze competition.

Will give you a "go" or "no go" answer about starting the business.

Table of Contents

Profile of competitors

Competitive advantage

Benefits to clients

4. Marketing/Sales Strategy

Income sources

Marketing strategy

Pricing

Advertising and Promotion

Sales Strategy

5. Research & Development

Patents, copyrights and brands

Product/Service Development

6. Staffing and Operations

Management Organization Charts

Staffing

Training Plans

Operations

7. Financial Projections

Key Assumptions

Profit and Loss Accounts

Balance Sheets

Cash-flow Projections

8. Sales Pipeline

9. Funding Requirements

10. Appendices

Confidentiality Agreement

The undersigned reader acknowledges that the information provided in this business plan is confidential; therefore, the reader agrees not to disclose it without the express written permission of <<Company/Promoter>>.

It is acknowledged by the reader that information to be furnished in this business plan is in all respects confidential in nature, other than information that is in the public domain through other means, and that any disclosure or use of this confidential information by the reader may cause serious harm or damage to <<Company>>.

Upon request, this document is to be immediately returned to <<Company/Promoter>>.

Signature

Name (printed)

Date

This is a business plan. It does not imply offering of securities.

1. Executive Summary

<< Introduce promoters here, and the reason you are now preparing this Business Plan.

This section should not be completed until the business plan is written. It will highlight all milestones in the company's development over the next five years. It should sum up the following areas:

- Purpose of the plan
- Product or service and its advantages
- Market opportunity
- Management team
- Track record, if any
- Financial projections
- Funding requirements

Financial projections should be summarized and highlighted. The following format is suggested as a guide:

	Year 1	Year 2	Year 3
Sales			
Exports			
Net Profit before Tax			
Investment			
Employment			

Remember that potential investors often make a provisional judgement based on the executive summary, and that their decision to read the main body of the business plan will depend on the information presented here. The appendices at the back of the plan contain more detailed information to support the main text of the business plan. >>

2. Company Description

Promoters and Shareholders

<< Description of the people involved in starting the business:

- Promoters
- Management structure and areas of responsibility

- Shareholders names, no. of shares, % shareholding and cash investment to date

Advisors

<< Financial, legal, and other advisors should be listed, with names, addresses and contact details. >>

Products and services

<< Explain clearly what your product or service is and what it does.

- Background to its development
- Benefits and Features
- Unique selling points
- Advantages to customers
- Disadvantages or weak points
- Future developments >>

Long Term Aim of the Business

<< State the long-term aim of the new business. >>

Objectives

<< State the specific milestones to be achieved by the company over the next five years (sales, exports, employment, product development, etc). >>

SWOT Analysis

<< Analyze the strengths and weaknesses of the business and product or service, the opportunities that exist in the marketplace, and the threats to the viability of the project. This is best done in a matrix diagram as follows:

3. Market Analysis

<< This section covers market research and competitor analysis. You must show that you have done the market research to justify the projections made in your business plan. It must demonstrate that there is a viable market and that you can beat the competition in the market for sales. >>

Target Market

<< The market to which you are planning to sell the product or service. Analyze the segments of this market as follows:

Size of each market segment
Is the segment growing or declining?
Characteristics of potential customers in each segment >>

Total Market Valuation

<< Show the total potential value of the market for this type of product or service, in all the targeted markets,

domestic and international. >>

Target Company revenue

<< These figures are the basis for the sales figures in your financial projections and must be based on realistic assessments. Include average deal size, length of sales cycle, recurring revenues>>

Market Trends

<< Analyze what is happening in the market:

Recent changes
Future predictions
Drivers such as demographic changes, economic and legislative factors
Implications for your product or service
Your plans to meet future demands and changes in the market >>

Profile of Competitors

<<Analysis of your competitors in the market:

What are the competing products and services?
Profile of key players (company size, turnover, profitability etc) and their market share
Advantages and disadvantages of the competitors' offerings
>>

Competitive Advantage

<< This is your assessment of why potential customers will choose to buy your product in place of those profiled above. Advantages may include:
Unique features
Price
New technologies or systems
Better value to customers in terms of efficiency or ROI or cost/benefit ratios
Greater compatibility with existing systems
Include any independent validation or case studies >>

Benefits to Clients

<< This is what your product or service provides to potential customers in terms of their own business goals. Does your product or service enable them to:
Increase sales
Increase efficiencies
Save money?
Save time?
Maximise resources?
Reduce errors?
Reduce downtime?
Improve Customer Service, reduce churn, increase loyalty

What will buying your product or service actually do for the customer? >>

4. Marketing/Sales Strategy

<< This section sets out your strategies for reaching your target market, arousing their interest in your product or service, and actually delivering the product or service to them in sales. >>

Marketing Strategy

<< How you will position your product or service in the market and differentiate it from its competitors:

Which segments of the market will be targeted first and why?

How will this be developed to reach the full target market?

How will you differentiate your product or service?

What key benefits will be highlighted?

What potential customers have you already targeted?

Have you a test site in operation, and what feedback is coming from this?

What contacts can be used to generate market awareness and sales?

Who will do the marketing: staff, agency, reps? >>

Revenue Sources

<< What contributions to revenue and profit will your business have?

	Irl	EU	US	Rest of World
Products				
Services				
Licenses				
After sales				
Upgrades				

Sales Strategy

<< How you will sell your product or service to the target market.

Directly
Retail
Distributor
Agent
Sales rep
Website
Revenue Sharing Partners

Analyze for each method the costs involved, whether it will reach the intended market efficiently, the control you would retain over the pricing and positioning, the logistics, and the overall integration with your marketing strategy. State the advantages of the methods you have chosen to sell your product or service. >>

Pricing

<< How you will set the price charged for your product or service. Considerations include:

Competitors' prices
Level of competition in the market
Perception of quality-price relationship by customers
Production costs and overheads
Chain of distribution and the added-value at each stage
The extent to which the buyer can control the price
State how each product or service will be priced, referring to the income sources above. >>

Marketing and Communications Strategy

<< How you will promote your product or service in the marketplace.

Advertising – where, when, how, to whom
Public relations
Direct marketing
Website and internet marketing
Exhibitions and conferences
Word of mouth >>

5. Research and Development

Technology Roadmap

<< Show the intended future development of your product or service, i.e., changes to meet future market demands, adaptations to international markets, or upgrades. Also detail plans for new products or services to add to the range.

Include
Team/Department structure
Methodology
Platforms used
Milestones to be achieved
System Overview Diagram>>

Research and Development

<< Indicate whether you will have ongoing R&D as an activity of the company, what areas this will be exploring and what future contributions to the company you expect from this research. >>

Technical Partners

<< List all partners and indicate nature of involvement >>

IP, Patents, Copyrights, Brands

<< Indicate any protection available for your product or service: whether the technology can be or has been patented, whether you can avail of copyright or trademark registration, and the brand image you intend to build up as a protection against competition. >>

6. Staffing and Operations

<< This is where you will outline the intended structure of the company in terms of management, number of employees, and the physical operational requirements to produce or supply the product or service. >>

Management (including Board) Organisation Chart

<< Include a diagram of the way in which the management of the new venture will be organized. This should show the areas of responsibility of each manager and the employees to be taken on over the next three years. >>

Staffing

<< State what employees will be taken on over the next three years, with which skills, in which areas of the business. >>

Training Plans

<< Outline the planned employee and management development to be undertaken in order to maintain a skilled workforce. This should also tie in with the future market developments and any new product or service developments. >>

Operations

<< State the physical requirements of the business:

- Premises
- Equipment
- Production facilities
- Infrastructure
- Communications facilities
- Costs involved
- Suppliers >>

7. Financial Projections

I   Key Assumptions
II   Profit and Loss Accounts
III   Balance Sheets
IV   Cashflow

Requirements for Preparation of Projections

1. Opening figures included based on latest Mgmt/Audited accounts

2. Shareholders Fund analyzed into Share Capital, Share Premium and Retained Profits

3. Sales Assumptions provided by unit, price segment & geography and reconciled to pipeline

4. Expenditure categorized into R&D, Admin and Overheads and Promoters / key managers salaries

5. Identification of monthly and cumulative company operational deficits

6. Sensitivity analysis may be required, detailing strategies to be implemented if sales or expenditure targets are not met.

7. Projections should identify separately Operational Cash Flow and external Cash Injections

I   Key Assumptions

<< This section reviews the key assumptions used in the financial projections. It is a guide to explain how key figures in the financial projections were arrived at. Included here should be items such as:

- Income sources
- Number of employees projected for each year and their intended salaries

- Projected investment in equipment and materials
- Projected R&D costs
- Depreciation allowed for
- Expected rent and rates charges
- Creditor days expected and debtor days allowed
- Expense calculations

This section should be brief and to the point. Further detail regarding these items can be placed in the Appendices. >>

II *Profit & Loss Accounts*

<< Attach here projected profit and loss accounts for the first three years of the company's operations. >>

III *Balance Sheets*

<< Attach here projected balance sheets for the first three years of the company's operations. >>

IV *Cashflow*

<< Attach here a monthly cashflow prediction for the first two years of the company's operations. >>

8. Sales Pipeline

Table as follows:

Name of Customer	Size of Deal	Date PO expected	Probability % of Getting Sale

9. Funding Requirements

<< State here the total funding requirements of the business, and how those are intended to be provided. You will also need to state the approximate breakdown of how these funds are to be spent.

Sources:

- Promoters' funds
- Bank lending
- Grants or loans from agencies
- Investment already received
- Investment sought

Required for:

- Equipment

- R&D
- Marketing
- Staffing >>

10. Appendices

<< This section is used to provide the detailed data on which the main text of the business plan is based, and to provide extra information of interest to the readers of the business plan. Items for inclusion in appendices vary from business to business, but normally include some of the following:

- Promoters' CVs
- Detailed financial assumptions
- Most recent Company Audited Accounts
- Share Cap table and Investment history
- Term Sheet from Potential Investors
- Detailed market research findings
- Promotional literature
- Product or service information
- Details of company website
- Testimonials or letters of intent from customers >>

4. How to Attract Investors

Venture capital financing is a method used for Raising Cash For Business and Getting Investments for Business, but less popular than borrowing. Venture capital firms, like banks, supply you with the funds necessary to operate your business, but they do it differently. Banks are creditors; they expect you to repay the borrowed money. Venture capital firms are owners; they hold stock in the company, adding their invested capital to its equity base. While banks may concentrate on cash flow, venture capital firms invest for long-term capital. Commonly, these firms look for their investment to appreciate three to five times in five or seven years.

One way of explaining the different ways in which banks and venture capital firms evaluate a small business seeking funds is: Banks look at its immediate future, but are most heavily influenced by its past; venture capitalists look to its longer run future.

To be sure, venture capital firms and individuals are interested in many of the same factors that influence bankers in their analysis of loan applications from smaller companies. All financial people want to know the results and ratios of past operations, the amount and intended use of the needed funds, and the earnings and financial condition of future projections.

But venture capitalists look much more closely at the features of the product and the size of the market than do commercial banks.

What Venture Capital Firms Look For (Raising Cash For Business)

Banks are creditors. They're interested in the product/market position of the company for assurance that this product or service can provide steady sales and generate sufficient cash flow to repay the loan. They look at projections to be certain that owners/managers have done their homework.

Venture capital firms are owners. They hold stock in the company, adding their invested capital to its equity base. Therefore, they examine existing or planned products or services and the potential markets for them with extreme care. They invest only in firms they believe can rapidly increase sales and generate substantial profits. The reason for this is that venture capital firms invest for long-term capital, not for interest income. A common estimate is that they look for three to five times their investment in five or seven years.

Of course, venture capitalists don't realize capital gains on all their investments. Certainly they don't make capital gains of 300 to 500% except on a very limited portion of their total investments. But their intent is to find venture projects with this appreciation potential to make up for investments that aren't successful.

Venture capital is risky due to the difficulty of judging the worth of a business in its early stages. Therefore, most venture capital firms set rigorous policies for venture proposal size, maturity of the seeking company, management of the seeking company, and "something special" in the plan that is submitted. They also have rigorous evaluation procedures to reduce risks, since their investments are unprotected in the event of failure.

Size of the Venture Proposal

Most venture capital firms are interested in investment projects requiring an investment of $250,000 to $1,500,000. Projects requiring under $250,000 are of limited interest because of the high cost of investigation and administration; however, some venture capital firms will consider smaller proposals if the investment is intriguing enough.

The typical venture capital firm receives over 400 proposals a year. Probably 90% of these will be rejected quickly because they don't fit the established geographical, technical or market area policies of the firm - or because they have been poorly prepared.

The remaining 10% are carefully investigated. These investigations are expensive. Firms may hire consultants to evaluate the product, particularly when it is the result of innovation or is technologically complex. The market size and competitive position of the company are analyzed by contacts with present and potential customers, suppliers, and others. Production costs are reviewed. The financial condition of the company is confirmed by an auditor. The legal form and registration of the business are checked. Most importantly, the character and competence of the management are evaluated by the venture capital firm, normally via a thorough background check.

These preliminary investigations may cost a venture firm between $2,000 and $3,000 per company investigated. They result in perhaps ten to fifteen proposals of interest. Then, second investigations, more thorough and more expensive than the first, reduce the number of proposals under consideration to only three or four. Eventually, the firm invests in one or two of these.

Most venture capital firms' investment interest is limited to projects proposed by companies with some operating history, even though they may not yet have shown a profit. Companies that can expand into a new product line or a new market with additional funds are particularly interesting. The venture capital firm can provide funds to enable such companies to grow in a spurt rather than gradually as they would on retained earnings. Raising Money From Investors.

Companies that are just starting or that have serious financial difficulties may interest some venture capitalists, if the potential for significant gain over the long run can be identified and assessed. If the venture firm has already extended its portfolio to a large risk concentration, they may be reluctant to invest in these areas because of increased risk of loss. Getting Investments for Business.

Although most venture capital firms will not consider a great many proposals from start-up companies, there are a small number of venture firms that will do "start-up" financing. The small firm that has a well thought-out plan and can demonstrate that its management group has an outstanding record (even if it is with other companies) has a decided edge in acquiring this kind of seed capital.

Most venture capital firms concentrate primarily on the competence and character of the management. They feel that even mediocre products can be successfully manufactured, promoted, and distributed by an experienced, energetic management group.

They look for a group that is able to work together easily and productively, especially under conditions of stress from temporary reversals and competition problems. Obviously, analysis of managerial skill is difficult. A partner or senior executive of a venture capital firm normally spends at least a week at the offices of a company being considered, talking with and observing the management to estimate their competence and character.

Venture capital firms usually require that the company under consideration have a complete management group. Each of the important functional areas product design, marketing, production, finance, and control - must be under the direction of a trained, experienced member of the group. Responsibilities must be clearly assigned. And, in addition to a thorough understanding of the industry, each member of the management team must be firmly committed to the company and its future. Raising Money From Investors.

Next in importance to the excellence of the management group, most venture capital firms seek a distinctive element in the strategy or product/market/process position of the company. This distinctive element may be a new feature of the product or process or a particular skill or technical competence of the management. But it must exist. It must provide a competitive advantage.

Elements of a Venture Proposal - Getting Investments for Business

Purpose and Objectives

Include a summary of the what and why of the project.

Proposed Financing: You must state the amount of money you will need from the beginning to the maturity of the project proposed, how the proceeds will be used, how you plan to structure the financing, and why the amount designated is required.

Marketing: Describe the market segment you've got or plan to get, the competition, the characteristics of the market, and your plans (with costs) for getting or holding the market segment you're aiming at.

History of the Firm: Summarize the significant financial and organizational milestones,

description of employees and employee relations, explanations of banking relationships, recounting of major services or products your firm has offered during its existence, and the like.

Description of the Product or Service: Include a full description of the product (process) or service offered by the firm and the costs associated with it in detail.

Financial Statements: Include statements for both the past few years and pro forma projections (balance sheets, income statements, and cash flows) for the next three to five years, showing the effect anticipated if the project is undertaken and if the financing is secured. (This should include an analysis of key variables affecting financial performance, showing what could happen if the projected level of revenue is not attained.)

Capitalization: Provide a list of shareholders, how much is invested to date, and in what form (equity/debt).

Biographical Sketches: Describe the work histories and qualifications of key owners and employees.

Principal Suppliers and Customers, Problems Anticipated and Other Pertinent Information

Provide a candid discussion of any contingent liabilities, pending litigation, tax or patent difficulties, and any other contingencies that might affect the project you're proposing. List the names, addresses and the

telephone numbers of suppliers and customers; they will be contacted to verify your statement about payments (suppliers) and products (customers).

Provisions of the Investment Proposal

What happens when, after the exhaustive investigation and analysis, the venture capital firms decides to invest in a company? Most venture firms prepare an equity financing proposal that details the amount of money to be provided, the percentage of common stock to be surrendered in exchange for these funds, the interim financing method to be used and the protective covenants to be included.

This proposal will be discussed with the management of the company. The final financing agreement will be negotiated and generally represents a compromise between the management of the company and the partners or senior executives of the venture capital firm. The important elements of this compromise are: ownership, control, annual charges, and final objectives.

Ownership

Venture capital financing is not inexpensive for the owners of a small business. The partners of the venture firm buy a portion of the business' equity in exchange for their investment.

This percentage of equity varies, of course, and depends on the amount of money provided, the success and worth of the business, and the anticipated investment return. It can range from perhaps 10% in the case of an established, profitable company to as much as 80 or 90% for beginning or financially troubled firms.

Most venture capital firms, at least initially, don't want a position of more than 30 to 40% because they want the owner to have the incentive to keep building the business. If additional financing is required to support

business growth, the outsiders' stake may exceed 50% but investors realize that small business owner/managers can lose their entrepreneurial zeal under those circumstances. In the final analysis, however, the venture firm, regardless of its percentage of ownership, really wants to leave control in the hands of the company's managers because it is really investing in that management team in the first place.

Most venture firms determine the ratio of funds provided to equity requested by a comparison of the present financial worth of the contributions made by each of the parties to the agreement. The present value of the contribution by the owner of a starting or financially troubled company is obviously rated low. Often it is estimated as just the existing value of his or her idea and the competitive costs of the owner's time. The contribution by the owners of a thriving business is valued much higher. Generally, it is capitalized at a multiple of the current earnings and/or net worth.

Financial valuation is not an exact science. The final compromise on the worth of the owner's contribution in the equity financing agreement is likely to be much lower than the owner thinks it should be and considerably higher than the partners of the capital firm think it might be. In the ideal situation, of course, the two parties to the agreement are able to do together what neither could do separately: 1) the company is able to grow fast enough with the additional funds to do more than overcome the owner's loss of equity; and 2) the investment grows at a sufficient rate to compensate the venture capitalists for assuming the risk.

An equity financing agreement with an outcome in five to seven years which pleases both parties is ideal. Since the parties cannot see this outcome in the present, neither will be perfectly satisfied with the compromise reached.

It is important, though, for the business owner to look at the future. He or she should carefully consider the impact of the ratio of funds invested to the ownership given up, not only for the present, but for the years to come.

Control

Control is a much simpler issue to resolve. Unlike the division of ownership over which the venture firm and management are likely to disagree, control is an issue in which they have a common interest. While it is understandable that the management of a small company will have some anxiety in this area, the partners of a venture firm have little interest in assuming control of the business. They have neither the technical nor the managerial personnel to run a number of small companies in diverse industries. They much prefer to leave operating control to the existing management.

The venture capital firm does, however, want to participate in any strategic decisions that might change the basic product/market character of the company and in any major investment decisions that might divert or deplete the financial resources of the company. They will, therefore, generally ask that at least one partner be made a director of the company.

They also want to be able to assume control and attempt to rescue their investment if severe financial, operating or marketing problems

develop. Thus, they will usually include protective covenants in their equity financing agreements to permit them to take control and appoint new officers if financial performance is very poor.

Annual Charges

The investment of the venture capital firm may be in the final form of direct stock ownership which does not impose fixed charges. More likely, it will be in an interim form - convertible subordinated debentures or preferred stock. Financings may also be straight loans with options or warrants that can be converted to a future equity position at a pre-established price.

The convertible debenture form of financing is like a loan. The debentures can be converted at an established ratio to the common stock of the company within a given period, so that the venture capital firm can prepare to realize their capital gains at their option in the future. These instruments are often subordinated to existing and planned debt to permit the company invested in to obtain additional bank financing.

Debentures also provide additional security and control for the venture firm and impose a fixed charge for interest (and possibly principal) on the company. The owner/manager of a small company seeking equity financing should consider the burden of any fixed annual charges resulting from the financing agreement.

Final Objectives

Venture capital firms generally intend to realize capital gains on their investments by providing for a stock buy-back by the small firm, by arranging a public offering of stock of the company invested in or by providing for a merger with a larger firm that has publicly traded stock. They usually hope to do this within five to seven years of their initial investment. (It should be noted that several additional stages of financing may be required over this period of time.)

Most equity financing agreements include provisions guaranteeing that the venture capital firm may participate in any stock sale or approve any merger, regardless of their percentage of stock ownership. Sometimes the agreement will require that the management work toward an eventual stock sale or merger. Clearly, the owner/manager of a small company seeking equity financing must consider the future impact upon his or her own stock holdings and personal ambition of the venture firm's aims, since taking in a venture capitalist as a partner may be virtually a commitment to eventually sell out or go public.

Types of Venture Capital Firms

Traditional Partnerships are often established by wealthy families to aggressively manage a portion of their funds by investing in small companies.

Professionally Managed Pools are made up of institutional money and which operate like the traditional partnerships.

Investment Banking Firms usually trade in more established securities, but occasionally form investor syndicates for venture proposals.

Insurance Companies often have required a portion of equity as a condition of their loans to smaller companies as protection against inflation.

Manufacturing Companies have sometimes looked upon investing in smaller companies as a means of supplementing their research and development programs.

In addition to these venture capital firms, there are individual private investors and finders. Finders, which can be firms or individuals, often know the capital industry and may be able to help the small company seeking capital to locate it, though they are generally not sources of capital themselves. Care should be exercised so that a small business owner deals with reputable, professional finders whose fees are in line with industry practice. Further, it should be noted that venture capitalists generally prefer working directly with principals in making investments, though finders may provide useful introductions.

The Importance of Formal Financial Planning

In case there is any doubt about the implications of the previous sections, it should be noted that it is extremely difficult for any small firm especially the starting or struggling company - to get venture capital.

There is one thing, however, that owner/managers of small businesses can do to improve the chances of their venture proposals at least escaping the 90% which are almost immediately rejected. In a word - plan.

Having financial plans demonstrates to venture capital firms that you are a competent manager, that you may have that special managerial edge over other small business owners looking for equity money. You may gain a decided advantage through well-prepared plans and projections that include: cash budgets, pro forma statements, and capital investment analysis and capital source studies.

Cash budgets should be projected for one year and prepared monthly.

They should combine expected sales revenues, cash receipts, material, labor and overhead expenses, and cash disbursements on a monthly basis. This permits anticipation of fluctuations in the level of cash and planning for short term borrowing and investment.

Pro forma statements should be prepared for planning up to three years ahead. They should include both income statements and balance sheets.

Again, these should be prepared quarterly to combine expected sales revenues; production, marketing and administrative expenses; profits; product, market or process investments; and supplier, bank or investment company borrowings. Pro forma statements permit you to anticipate the financial results of your operations and to plan intermediate term borrowings and investments.

Capital investment analyses and capital source studies should be prepared for planning up to five years ahead. The investment analyses should compare rate of return for product, market, or process investment, while the source alternatives should compare the cost and availability of debt and equity and the expected level of retained earnings, which together will support the selected investments. These analyses and source studies should be prepared quarterly so you may anticipate the financial consequences of changes in your company's strategy. They will allow you to plan long term borrowings, equity placements, and major investments.

There is a bonus in making such projections. They force you to consider the results of your actions. Your estimates must be explicit; you have to examine and evaluate your managerial records; disagreements must be resolved - or at least discussed and understood. Financial planning may be burdensome but it is one of the keys to business success.

Now, making these financial plans will not guarantee that you'll be able to get venture capital. Not making them will virtually assure that you won't receive favorable consideration from venture capitalists.

5. Special Free Bonuses (download links are provided)

a. MS Word format version of the business plan template identical to the one in chapter of this book - Extensive business plan template in MS word format - this is a high quality, full blown business plan template complete with detailed instructions and all related spread sheets. Allows you to prepare a professional business plan.

Copy the following link to your browser and save the file to your PC:

http://www.bizmove.com/tools/Startup-Business-Plan-Template.docx

b. Excel Financial Projections Creator - simply type in your business' details and assumptions and it will automatically produce a comprehensive set of financial projections for your specific business, including: Start-Up Expenses, Projected Balance Sheet, Projected Cash Flow Statement, Financial Ratios Analysis, Projected Profit and Loss Statement, Break Even Analysis, and many more.

Copy the following link to your browser and save the file to your PC:

http://www.bizmove.com/bp/projections.xlsx

c. Detailed guide that will walk you step by step and show you exactly how to effectively use the above Excel Financial Projections Creator.

Copy the following link to your browser and save the file to your PC:

http://www.bizmove.com/bp/projections-guide.doc

d. Simple business plan template in MS Word format - allows you to craft a good business plan quickly and easily.

Copy the following link to your browser and save the file to your PC:

http://www.bizmove.com/tools/bptemplate.docx

e. How to Improve Your Leadership and Management Skills (eBook) - Discover powerful strategies to motivate and inspire your people to bring out the best in them. Be the boss people want to give 200 percent for.

Copy the following link to your browser and save the file to your PC:

http://www.bizmove.com/bp/leadership.pdf

f. Small Business Management: Essential Ingredients for Success (eBook) - Learn effective business management tricks, secrets and shortcuts to make your business a success.

Copy the following link to your browser and save the file to your PC:

http://www.bizmove.com/bp/management.pdf

g. Business Plan Training Course (Online Video)

This training course discusses the creation of a business plan. It explains the importance of business planning, defines and describes the business plan outline and its components thus enabling you to develop a very good business plan.

Copy the following link to your browser and save the file to your PC:

http://www.bizmove.com/video//business-plan-training-course.htm

g. How To Find And Attract Investors Training Course (Online Video):

This self-paced training video will show you how to find and attract investors. Topics include determining the need for outside financing, defining what an investor is and where to find them, explaining the investment process and understanding investor expectations.

Copy the following link to your browser and save the file to your PC:

http://www.bizmove.com/business-training/how-to-find-and-attract-investors.htm.

Printed in Great Britain
by Amazon